W9-APD-071

# STRONGEST ANIMALS

## That's Wild!
### A Look at Animals

Big Buddy BOOKS
That's Wild!

ABDO
Publishing Company

Julie Murray

## VISIT US AT
### www.abdopublishing.com

Published by ABDO Publishing Company, 8000 West 78th Street, Edina, Minnesota 55439.

Copyright © 2010 by Abdo Consulting Group, Inc. International copyrights reserved in all countries. No part of this book may be reproduced in any form without written permission from the publisher. Buddy Books™ is a trademark and logo of ABDO Publishing Company.

Printed in the United States of America, North Mankato, Minnesota.
112009
012010

 PRINTED ON RECYCLED PAPER

Coordinating Series Editor: Rochelle Baltzer
Editor: Sarah Tieck
Contributing Editors: Heidi M.D. Elston, Megan M. Gunderson, BreAnn Rumsch, Marcia Zappa
Graphic Design: Deborah Coldiron, Maria Hosley
Cover Photograph: *Eighth Street Studio*; *iStockphoto*: ©iStockphoto.com/DeMoN89, ©iStockphoto.com/Rouzes.
Interior Photographs/Illustrations: *Eighth Street Studio* (pp. 11, 13, 15, 22, 30); *iStockphoto*: ©iStockphoto.com/
archives (p. 5), ©iStockphoto.com/ChrisHepburn (p. 11), ©iStockphoto.com/ddea (p. 29), ©iStockphoto.com/
Jbryson (p. 25) ©iStockphoto.com/mammamaart (p. 29); *Minden Pictures*: Mathias Breiter (p. 20); *Peter Arnold, Inc.*: ©Biosphoto/Fischer Berndt (p. 27), ©Biosphoto/Klein J.-L&Hubert M. -L (p. 9), ©Biosphoto/Hazan Muriel
(p. 23), Steffen Honzera (p. 7), WILDLIFE (pp. 5, 24), Gunter Ziesler (p. 24); *Shutterstock*: Andrjuss (p. 11),
Angel's Gate Photography (p. 7), Wesley Aston (p. 5), Steven Bower (p. 9), FloridaStock (p. 23), Jacek Jasinski
(p. 15), Geoffrey Kuchera (p. 29), Mayskyphoto (p. 29), orionmystery@flickr (p. 17), Niels Quist (p. 12), Dr.
Morley Read (pp. 5, 18), wupeng (p. 17), Anke van Wyk (p. 5).

### Library of Congress Cataloging-in-Publication Data

Murray, Julie, 1969-
  Strongest animals / Julie Murray.
     p. cm. -- (That's wild! A look at animals)
  ISBN 978-1-60453-981-3
  1. Animal physiology--Juvenile literature. 2. Muscles--Juvenile literature.  I. Title.
  QP321.M87 2010
  590--dc22
                                    2009034358

# Contents

# Wildly Strong!

Many amazing animals live in our world. Some are big and others are small. They may fly, run, or swim.

Some animals are wildly strong! Their strength helps them survive in their **habitats**. Being strong might help them catch meals or lift heavy objects. Let's learn more about strong animals!

Grizzly Bears

Pacific Ocean

Leaf-cutter Ants

4

Strong animals live all over the world. The same type of animal may live in several parts of the world.

Harpy Eagle

North America

Europe

Asia

Atlantic Ocean

Africa

South America

Indian Ocean

Gorilla

Antarctica

African Elephant

5

# Now, That's Hungry!

African elephants are big, strong animals. Males can weigh nearly 15,000 pounds (6,800 kg)! These mighty animals push over trees so they can eat the tree parts.

Elephants have **muscular** trunks. An elephant can lift about 550 pounds (250 kg) with its trunk! It uses its trunk to pick up objects and spray water.

Sometimes, elephants may push over trees simply to test their strength!

An African elephant can knock down trees that are up to 30 feet (9 m) tall and two feet (1 m) wide.

7

# Bear-y Strong

Grizzly bears live in North America. They have **muscular** bodies. When they stand on two legs, many are more than six feet (2 m) tall. Most males weigh more than 500 pounds (230 kg)!

Grizzly bears often eat plants and berries. But, they can use their strength to attack **prey**. One hit from a grizzly's powerful arm could knock down a moose!

Grizzly bears can attack and eat animals as large as moose. Some grizzlies even pick up their prey and carry it off.

Moose are large animals. On average, they weigh 800 to 1,400 pounds (360 to 640 kg).

9

# Big Mussels

Mussels may just look like shells. But, these water animals are known for their strength.

Mussels have **muscles** that keep their shells closed tight. Their shells **protect** them from predators, such as starfish and birds.

10

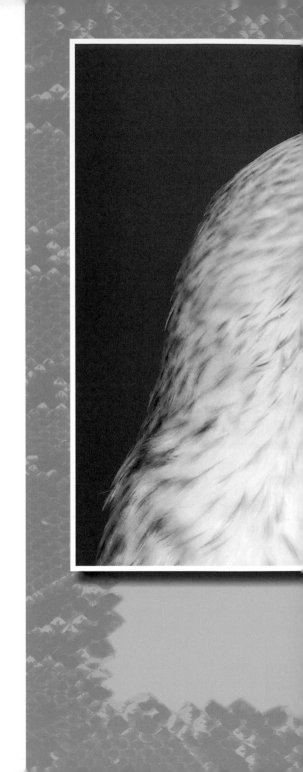

Seagulls pick up mussels (*above*) and drop them on hard surfaces to crack their shells. Then, they eat the soft bodies inside the shells (*right*).

Byssus threads help mussels attach to objects or other mussels.

Mussels are also known for **attaching** themselves to objects, such as rocks. Many mussels produce byssus threads. These strong threads keep mussels secure in rough waters. Mussels can hold on so tight it seems like they are stuck on!

## Home Sweet Home

Freshwater mussels often live on rocks and sand on the bottoms of rivers, lakes, and streams. Marine mussels live in shallow water along ocean coasts.

13

# Strong Arm

Gorillas are the world's largest ape. Adult gorillas have big, **muscular** chests. Their arms are longer than their legs. A gorilla's upper body is believed to be about six times stronger than an adult human's!

Though gorillas can climb trees, they live mostly on the ground. Their strength helps them bend and break tree branches for their nests.

Male gorillas can weigh more than 400 pounds (180 kg). Female gorillas grow about half that size.

14

**Aha!**

Gorillas live in Africa in jungles and mountains. They eat plants.

# Ant-tastic

Tiny ants are famous for their strength. An ant's body is small and lightweight. So, its **muscles** don't have to work hard to support its body. Instead, they are used to carry food and baby ants.

In place of bones, an ant has a hard shell called an exoskeleton. It is hollow, lightweight, and very strong. It supports the ant's weight and **protects** its inner body parts.

Sometimes ants work as a team to carry heavy objects.

Ants have a mouthpart called a mandible. It allows them to lift objects.

17

18

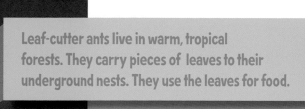

Leaf-cutter ants live in warm, tropical forests. They carry pieces of leaves to their underground nests. They use the leaves for food.

The biggest ants are about the size of a paper clip. But, all ants can carry heavy objects. Many scientists believe leaf-cutter ants can lift more than ten times their body weight!

Salmon can jump waterfalls
as high as ten feet (3 m)!

# Jump! Jump!

Salmon are known for their swimming skills. When it is time to **spawn**, they return to their birthplace. This may be hundreds of miles upstream.

Still, salmon make the journey. They swim against fast-moving river water. Sometimes, salmon must leap over **rapids** and waterfalls! This is hard work, but their bodies are very strong.

# Eagle Eye

Eagles are strong birds. Their bodies are built to hunt and catch **prey**. Eagles have **muscular** feet with sharp claws called talons. They use these to catch prey.

Most eagles can carry prey that weighs almost as much as they do. But usually, eagles hunt smaller animals.

22

## They Get Around

Eagles live all over the world, except in Antarctica and New Zealand.

When an eagle catches an animal, it can pick it up and fly away.

23

Eagles have large, powerful wings. A harpy (*above*) and Philippine (*right*) eagle's wings stretch out about six feet (2 m) from tip to tip!

Two of the biggest eagles are the harpy eagle and the Philippine eagle. Both live in the treetops of **tropical** forests.

These powerful eagles eat small **mammals** and snakes. They may even eat monkeys! In fact, the Philippine eagle is also called the monkey-eating eagle.

# World's Strongest

Scientists believe the strongest creature on Earth is the rhinoceros beetle. This bug is small enough to fit into a person's hand. But, it can carry up to 850 times its own weight! That would be like an elephant lifting about 460 school buses!

Rhinoceros beetles live in tropical forests. Their strength helps them move through dirt, leaves, and other things on the forest floor.

27

# That WAS Wild!

From **muscular** gorillas to mighty ants, there are some very strong wild animals. Each of them is an important part of the animal kingdom.

People work hard to **protect** animals and their surroundings. You can help, too! Recycling and using less water are two simple things you can do. The more you learn, the more you can do to help keep animals safe.

Hiking on established trails helps protect wild animal homes.

People can work together to keep natural areas in their community clean.

Gorillas are in danger. Their homes are disappearing as cities grow. And, humans sometimes hunt them for meat or sport.

# Wow! Is That TRUE?

🐾 Giant anacondas are strong snakes. They can be 30 feet (9 m) long. Giant anacondas catch and eat animals as large as jaguars!

🐾 Oxen are very strong animals. In the 1800s, settlers used them to pull loaded wagons across the United States.

🐾 Some gorillas can be trained to use sign language.

# Important Words

**attach** to bind or join together.

**habitat** a place where a living thing is naturally found.

**mammal** a group of living beings. Mammals have hair and make milk to feed their babies.

**muscles** (MUH-suhls) body tissues, or layers of cells, that help move the body. Something with strong, well-developed muscles is muscular.

**prey** an animal hunted or killed by a predator for food.

**protect** (pruh-TEHKT) to guard against harm or danger.

**rapids** fast-moving parts of a river. Rocks or logs often break the surface of the water in these areas.

**spawn** to produce eggs.

**tropical** relating to an area on Earth where it is hot all year.

# Web Sites

To learn more about strong animals, visit ABDO Publishing Company online. Web sites about strong animals are featured on our Book Links page. These links are routinely monitored and updated to provide the most current information available.

## www.abdopublishing.com

# Index